Shaker House Poems

by Lyn Lifshin

sagarin press chatha

new york

Published in 1976 by
Sagarin Press
Chatham, N.Y. 12037

Copyright 1976 by Lyn Lifshin
All Rights Reserved

ISBN: 0-915298-02-3
Library of Congress Catalog Number: 74-24535

Printed in The United States by The Studley Press, Inc.

1

the first room
smells like wood

wooden wardrobe cherry
the wood polished
plain except what's
painted blue blue
buttermilk pan oval
box blue bench
200 years but
the fingers that
mixed powder for this
blue the woman
turning from a
man's fingers, hips

cases of medicine herbs
dried basil poppy
wormwood tansy thyme dark
hot cupboards full of
dry leaves pods

papery berries
night sitting around a table
labelling roots
pearls of chlorophyll pearls
of ether

living as brother and sister
slippery elm compound
of sasparilla

strainers sieves jugs
with painted blue wings

but so many pills for
torpid liver sick head
ache constipation dyspepsia

huge boxes Shaker Seeds
in bold letters the
first packaged seeds

red beets lavender
2000 lbs of seeds

Wove huge baskets to carry
in the grass
herbs and petals
dark purple gooseberry blood

fingers deep in the
moist dark pulling

Did they talk to the leaves
as if they were children
to get the
largest cucumbers
the biggest strawberry

4

room full of things
to clean with whistles
broom flannel broom
broom for inside
outside copper
kettles glistening
A room of tubs presses
irons racks screw
press for smoothing
sheets and pillows
knife edge folds
on the sheets they
lay down in
alone touch
the smooth white

days of scrubbing
pounding 14 women
ran this washing
press dreaming of
a white clean
as new snow

5

in this room

lemon sun
apples large
chopping block
marble churners

Coming into the warm kitchen
leek soup simmering

apples hanging to dry

Feeling the hot bricks thru
a cotton apron Warm
thighs Nights

stirring molasses

before the cool stiff sheets

small bed in a room
like a boat wood
ceiling cherry
table deep
blue threads

Some woman standing
near the plain
wood cupboard

drifts past the
bed clothes brooms

to a house of velvet
crystal the jade

Nights she couldn't
sleep or care

From this window the
corn in the moon
her eyes in the small
mirror Smell of
wet earth Stars
thru the lilac

long table with
vases silver

pale light on the
grain the
thatched chairs
worn where the legs
would bend Quiet

room with baskets
3 cats could live
in old

wood pine cherry
the original stain

Blue english bombay
small glasses for wine

Men and woman feeling
light on their backs
bent their heads together

"gather up the fragments
that remain that
nothing be lost"

lilac thru glass bees green

bibles bootracks

green curtains
green light on the
bed a photograph of

someone too pale
to see the

man living in this
room made the desk
of pine (so many
drawers

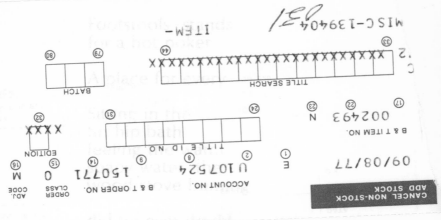

that he was in his

this room for
the children
their parents

it feels like
water blue
flowers

braiding spinning
reading straight

wood rockers bent
wood rockers
rockers with
spindleback the
men and women
singing together

samplers in their
blood stitched
don't touch

10

photographs of the
sisters dancing to
god the men joining

flinging their arms
and asses shouting
for joy shaking

shaking didn't
david and miriam
dance and sing
for the lord

Some danced so hard
they didn't know who
they were where

but they never touched

11

women counted

hoed and shovelled
snow made the rules

One sister could turn
3 thousand times and
not get dizzy the

next morning dig as
many potatoes as a man

first just the elders could carry watches

later spring or balance clocks
carried thru the trees

big clocks everywhere
hall clocks wall clocks

alarm bells to set
the other clocks

clocks with hymns painted inside
tower clocks on a
80 lb brass bell

No one could sign his name
on what he made

just on clocks

one day in august
a class of girls 10
to 14 suddenly started
shaking and whirling
Again in the evening
Even adults started
having gift visions
mansions in the sky
meetings with strange
people dead brothers
indians no one could
sleep or work right

dancing got so wild
one sunday they shut
the door for years
Gifts of love gold
jewels hymns and
rules prophecies
Many came in an
unkown tongue
were assumed to be
indian until un
known tongues
were forbidden

windchimes aeolian harps

groves of tulips

one sunday in may
in october

dancing around the
fountain stone

smell of sun on their faces

dancing till they fall in the grass

Changed the names of cities
hancock the city
of peace its feast
place mt. sinai

waterveliet: wisdom's valley
valley of bliss

They said they wanted to die in
the body to be reborn

went home with grass stains, starved

no time on the sundial

hot and grey leaning
against red clapboard

thunder somewhere
coming hot grass
She smoothes her hair
smells the new cotton

learning what herbs
heal lemon thyme
sage rosemary

rue she
closes her eyes

lets a man come
closer touch her
lips inside her
thigh Wakes
her skin burning
wondering how long
this will go on

16

listen have you
ever heard of

i won't take your
mumbo jumbo

will wear
pantaloons

so no damn cow
can kick up my
skirt and
look she tells
them 70
years ago

indian baskets whips

notes chalked on black
boards black
books maps hours

in straight-backed chairs

(no names no
letters carved on
the wood they
loved wood

Slow hot afternoons
feeling the cool metal desk
leg whispering
about those 2
who would be
sleeping in the
same bed touching
everywhere

18

late afternoon december the

snow piling higher

cake and spice

women splitting poplar
wood into sticks
into shavings

small carved birds
for children
growing in their fingers

bells

19

cherry maple oak pine

pieces of heartwood

chips fall like hail

Men making frames
cabinets benches
chairs this
stove No

one looks up

no one notices the rain

stoned on
the beauty of wood

what the hands can do for love

hair undone alone
in the small room
curled with a
foot warmer
quilt pine
cones burning

writing about
rubies emeralds
jade stones she'd
never put on
her finger

hammers crashing
the hot forge

scream of horses

when i
first came
he says to the
stranger pulling
the leather gently

i didn't know it
wouldn't be
just for the day

their strange clothes,
ways but the

air was so clear
and i started
seeing things

it's been
50 years

wind blowing red
maple leaves into the
gravestones a

thin girl on a
swing pumping as if
to fly over the
dark hill

remembers living
in a city the
smell of perfume

tells a story of
an infant girl her
brother brought to
a place like this
their father dying
enroute to indiana

18 years and they
run off south her
bonnet on an
elm branch

tells this to
the wind hears
it echo

23

4 a.m.
pulling on
heavy cotton

looking away
from the mirror
as if guilty
for rubbing
her cheeks

dark steps
to the kitchen

peeling potatoes

a boy 16 too making
the fire waiting
his blue eyes
haunting her
This is as far
as it goes

As if to marry
or touch was
greed for
private property

24

in one case

needles gloves

worn slippers lined
with fleece they
raised flax in
cherry valley
wove raised
their silk worms

pink silk scarf
this blue one

bone and ivory
buttons no
rings

a wedding handkerchief

sampler stitched
i shall not want

If they'd just married

ice harvester

fleece still warm
from the sun

daffodils boiling
in a pot for yellow

sumac leaves
butternut
Looms

dancing with
linen silk
with flannel the

threads pulling
together

Women a
room of them
stoned on this
beauty from
their fingers

lives like their
chairs simple
functional

a taste for
primary colors
for using
pieces

living like wheels in
a delicate machine
they loved

Colophon

This the first trade edition
of Shaker House Poems was printed
offset from the special limited
edition of 110 copies by Leonard
Seastone of Tideline Press. This
edition is 1000 copies.